Why Can't My Life Be a Summer Vacation?

Early Teen Devotionals
by Kevin Johnson

Can I Be a Christian Without Being Weird?

Why Is God Looking For Friends?

Who Should I Listen To?

Why Can't My Life Be a Summer Vacation?

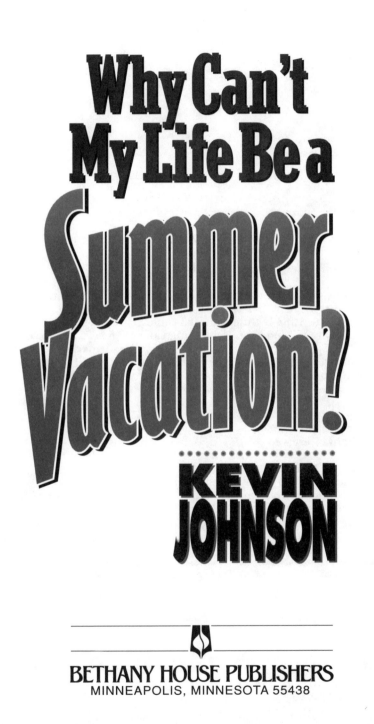

Why Can't My Life Be a Summer Vacation?

KEVIN JOHNSON

BETHANY HOUSE PUBLISHERS
MINNEAPOLIS, MINNESOTA 55438

Published by Bethany House Publishers
A Ministry of Bethany Fellowship, Inc.
11300 Hampshire Avenue South
Minneapolis, Minnesota 55438

Printed in the United States of America

Library of Congress Cataloging-in-Publication Data

CIP applied for

ISBN 1–55661–284–2   CIP

To Karin

Jesus has called you by name
You are His

KEVIN JOHNSON is an associate pastor at Elmbrook Church in metro Milwaukee, where he works with almost 400 sixth–eighth graders. While his training includes an M.Div. from Fuller Theological Seminary and a B.A. in English and Print Journalism from the University of Wisconsin at River Falls, his current interests run along the lines of cycling, in-line skating, books, guitar, and shortwave radio. Kevin and his wife, Lyn, live in Wisconsin with their two children, Nathaniel and Karin.

Contents

Part 3: Hitting the Wall

Part 4: Braving the Heat

PART 1

Going

for

GOLD

1
Where's the Finish Line?

A herd of cows glanced up from munching brunch to stare at the eighth graders cycling down their bumpy road. The cows were completely content. The bikers were crabby.

"Stopping!" Tom screeched from the back of the line. Everyone regrouped on the side of the road. "Something's wrong. I've clocked eight miles since that last left turn. Shouldn't we be to another road by now? Hey Eric—did you get us lost again?"

"Me? Don't blame me! You've got a map too." No one had noticed a turn, so they kept peddling until they reached the right road.

Miles later Katie yelled, "Stopping!"

"Why are we stopping this time?"

"Jon's barfing in the bushes. He can't take the heat."

"Ryan, you lied to us," Jennifer whined to the group leader. "You said this would be fun. We should have camped someplace where we could lie on the beach."

Late in the afternoon the riders pulled up at a store for snacks. After the break no one wanted to ride again: "I can't ride any further." "No more hills." "I busted my rear."

During the break Eric had been figuring. "Did anybody add up these distances on the map? We should have been done an hour ago, and we've still got thirty miles to go. After all our wrong turns and Jon's barf break we won't make it before dark."

As the group argued what to do, another group rode up and crumpled on the ground. "Shouldn't we be there by now?" one asked. "Where's the finish line?"

Knowing where and when you'll finish keeps you from quitting a tough ride. When ice-cold sodas, crystal lakes, frisbee time, and a soft sleeping bag wait for you, you can endure a lot. If you aren't sure that each push on the pedals propels you closer to the goal, you'll ditch the ride. Sweat for nothing, and you'll find something better to do.

If as a Christian the finish line seems out of reach or the ride harder than you expected, you'll quit.

Christians without a destination are like bikers wandering the countryside asking cows for directions. Christians lured off the route by attractive side trips never reach the finish line. Christians unprepared for bumps sooner or later *fwang* over their handlebars. And Christians focused only on the hard parts of being a Christian never think to enjoy the wind as they blow downhill.

This book will help you spot the goal, strengthen your legs, bust the ride, and brush the flies from your eyes. To use this book, read a chapter at a sitting—one a day if you can. Bring a Bible that's easy to read—you'll need it to look up Bible passages where it says 📑 **Read**. At the end of each chapter are a few verses you'll want to mull over or memorize to help you pedal harder.

Being a Christian isn't always an easy ride. But knowing Who awaits you at the finish line is worth every grunt and groan.

2
The Best Buy in the Megamall

Heather opened the front door, then wished she had looked through the peephole to see what was standing on her step. Too late now. She locked the screen door.

A man in a lime green leisure suit stepped forward with a dismal "Hullo. We're from the Church of the Bozos down the block."

The lady with him wore a dress that resembled the curtains in Heather's grandma's house. She looked as if the tight bun in her hair had cut off blood to her brain. It had. "Oh, honey, let me talk to her." She pushed her husband to the side. "Would you like a balloon, little girl?" she asked.

"Do I look like I do balloons?" Heather snapped back. "Hey, you haven't been over to my grandma's, have you?" The couple stood looking stupid until a boy Heather's age poked his head around. He was a three-quarter-size replica of his dad, to the suit.

"You're *my* age!" he squealed. "Will you come to church? *Pleeeeeease?*"

▶ **Read Matthew 13:44–46. Why did the digger swap everything he had for a treasure, and the merchant everything for a pearl?**

Your world has more salespeople than a megamall. Each tries to sell you something intended to make you totally goofy with happiness.

God isn't selling anything. What He offers is free: He wants to give you the gift of His friendship, greatness, presence, and guidance. He wants to be King of your life. Yet He lets you shop around, to choose for or against Him, to love Him or leave Him. Bozos, though, don't exactly help God's pitch. If you think being a Christian means becoming a Bozo, then you'll keep malling for a better deal.

But once you understand what God has for you—becoming part of the kingdom of heaven, knowing and following God—no one has to beg or force you to accept God's treasure. Nothing makes you say "Blecchhh!" or "No thanks!"

Following God won't make you weird. Christians just put trust and obedience to God first. Always. No matter what.

That's a price. But if you pay the price you'll forget what you gave up. What you had before is nothing compared to what you gain.

The kingdom of heaven is like treasure hidden in a field. When a man found it, he hid it again, and then in his joy went and sold all he had and bought that field.

MATTHEW 13:44

3
Earthshake

Play parent: Your family is buying a house. You must choose from a catalog featuring the only two houses for sale on the entire planet. House A has striking features: a gigantic sunken living room and a party-ready pool and deck in back. The contract for House A says specifically, however, that one day an earthquake will shake House A to the ground, with its owner in it. Nothing will be left—no house, no stuff, no you. No lie.

The drains in House B, a more modest dwelling, occasionally need unclogging, but the house promises to keep you snug and warm. Parts of the contract for House B, though, are tough to understand. It states that from time to time the house miraculously sprouts new rooms. And here's the strangest part: House B ultimately will be completely renovated and transported to an oceanside location at an unspoiled Malibu.

You're in charge of the family dollar. Which house would you choose?

Read Hebrews 12:22–29. What will survive when God shakes the world? ("They" in verse 25 refers to Israel, mentioned back in verses 14–21.)

You wouldn't be a happy home buyer if you moved into a house and found yourself stuck with mildewed living room carpet, a leaky pool, and a termite-infested deck. You would regret you hadn't examined the house up close. You would be in one ugly mood when the house shook to toothpicks and you hadn't believed that the purchase contract was legal, binding, and unalterable.

So don't buy a house God has said He will destroy.

God promises to share a home with believers where you can rock with the angel choir and room with non-bozos, where you're eternally welcome because Christ paid the bills and invited you in.

Living in God's house are the people who accepted Christ's gift (John 1:12). Living at the only other address in the universe are people who laugh at God's warning and refuse God's invitation to live with Him. When God shakes all of creation—to keep what's worth keeping—only God's house (and those in it) will stand strong. The other house—sin, and everyone in it—will be demolished.

Sound scary? Not if you choose the right house.

———————

Therefore, since we are receiving a kingdom that cannot be shaken, let us be thankful, and so worship God acceptably with reverence and awe, for our God is a consuming fire.

HEBREWS 12:28–29

4

If You Snooze You Lose

Just as Matt slapped the snooze button on his alarm clock (for the third time) his mom knocked on his bedroom door and hollered to see if he was awake. "It's eight o'clock, Matthew. We leave for church in half an hour."

By the time Matt dragged himself into the kitchen he was ready to whine. "Why do we have to do this? Can't we take a few Sundays off? You and Dad should go to church by yourselves. You like it." Matt thought Sunday school was okay. He just goofed around with his friends while the teacher droned on. And on. And on. But a second hour in worship service drove him crazy. Matt's parents weren't amused by his organ imitation—moaning like a cow in labor—and Matt couldn't figure out why the preacher got so worked up about everything.

One of these days, he told himself, *they're going to let me stay home.*

Read Colossians 1:9–14. Why would someone want to "please God in every way"?

Before we decide to trust God we think He's an overpriced pearl. We calculate that the treasure of knowing, following, and enjoying God ranks in value right up there with a coffee can of trinkets buried in the back-yard. So instead of recognizing God as King of the Universe, we rule our own lives. That makes us God's enemies, rebels against Him. We live far from Him, as residents of the "kingdom of darkness."

God says that His enemies have chosen death (Romans 6:23), a permanent address a long way from Him. But God figured out a way to move us back to Him. Though we deserve to die for our sins, Christ suffered our punishment. He died on the cross in our place so we can be forgiven (Colossians 1:21–23). God makes us citizens of the "kingdom of light" when we say to Him, *I've been wrong, God. I thought you weren't worth it. I disobeyed you. I accept the gift of forgiveness and life you offer through Christ.*

There's a reason real Christians act like real Christians. They decide daily to follow God because they've already made a bigger decision to trust Him—not just to believe *in* Him, but *believe Him,* that what He says is true and right.

God's gift is a strange one. It's not something you can put on a shelf. It's more like He signed you up for a race, paid your entry fee, and now you're at the starting line.

For he has rescued us from the dominion of darkness and brought us into the kingdom of the Son he loves, in whom we have redemption, the forgiveness of sins.

COLOSSIANS 1:13–14

18

5

On Your Mark

You waddle to the line for the 10,000 meter race wearing generously padded hockey bibs. You eyeball the runners next to you through your helmet's face cage. *Why is everyone dressed funny?* You struggle to bend over to take your mark, catching yourself with your thick gloves as you topple into position.

The starting gun fires. As you shuffle off and your blades slice into the dirt track you observe that it's hard to run in skates. And as the pack of runners pulls away, you look down and detect one more problem. You laced your skates together.

☑ **Read Hebrews 12:1–3. How should you dress for a race?**

You don't slog off on a long run in bibs, jersey, pads, gloves, helmet, and skates. That gear is great if you want to jam on ice. But it makes you a clod if you're running a race. If you hope to run well, you strip to essentials and slip on the lightest shoes you can find.

As Christians we have a race marked out for us, with an eternity in heaven with God and His people on the far side of the finish line. Our racecourse—a life lived in sync with God—isn't a short sprint. It's a long-distance run that demands focus and determination.

To run well we toss off anything not necessary for the race.

Sometimes, though, we lumber along with loads as out of place as hockey gear at a track meet—like a party calendar that crowds out time with Christian friends, or a sports schedule too busy for time alone with God.

Even worse is when we sin. Doing wrong leaves us wadded in a knot and sprawled on the track until we ask God for forgiveness and let Him pick us up.

We all show up wearing skates to the track meet. We have a lot of coaches, though—others whose lives we can learn from, believers who have run before (the "great cloud of witnesses" described in Hebrews 12). And we have Jesus, who ran better than anyone, to give us pointers.

. . . let us throw off everything that hinders and the sin that so easily entangles, and let us run with perseverance the race marked out for us.

HEBREWS 12:1B

20

6
The Finest Things in Life

The contents of Shawna's closet were spread out on her bed as she plotted partywear with Charise over the phone. "I don't know. Sweaters make me look pudgy—especially with a turtleneck. Huh? I can't wear *that*. I'll never wear that again. Don't you remember? The last time I did David called me 'bubble butt'. . . . Sure, I suppose. We could both kind of dress up. That would really make Jill look bad. . . . Yeah, I guess. The green outfit would be okay. Yeah, I know. It's kind of cute. You don't think it makes me look like a leprechaun, do you? I don't want anyone to laugh at me this time."

Read Matthew 6:25–34. What goal should you keep in the front of your mind?

Girls aren't the only ones who get intense about their wardrobes and clothes aren't the only things in life that can consume us. The problem? Hunting down the ultimate skate wheels, banking wads by babysitting, drilling to make the all-city soccer team, memorizing reruns of your favorite TV show, or mastering the six-hundred-and-forty-third level of your favorite video game—all these things aren't bad, but they can squeeze the best out of your brain.

You *need* clothes and food and a few other things.

You *want* fun and money and lots of other things. God wants to get your brain beyond that, to help you think about bigger things. Jesus says to seek *first* God's kingdom and righteousness.

To seek God's kingdom is to welcome God's reign in your life—to want what He wants. That's giving God your heart. To seek His righteousness is to look for ways to love Him and others. That's giving God your life.

When you run hard and fast after God He promises to take care of everything else: "All these things will be given to you as well."

That doesn't mean you never think about those other things. Birds dig worms and flowers drink, and it's not a bad idea for people to lay out clothes for the next day so they aren't late for school. But you don't need to huff yourself breathless figuring out what to buy or eat or play. You're running toward the wrong goal if you perpetually panic about what to wear without ever pondering how to live.

———————

For the pagans run after all these things, and your heavenly Father knows that you need them. But seek first his kingdom and his righteousness, and all these things will be given to you as well.

Matthew 6:32–33

7

Waves Gone Gonzo

After loafing too long on the beach Cassie started to name the seagulls that begged for lunch. While her friends surfed and swam and boogieboarded, Cassie twirled her toes in the sand and frequented the hot dog stand. Cassie wouldn't go in the water. She knew how to swim, but hadn't grown up on the ocean like her friends had. Waves terrified her.

Until her friends finally threw her in.

Waaaaaah! she howled as a wave whapped her. *Woaaaaaah!* she laughed as she figured out how to bob to the top. *Haaaaaaaaah!* Cassie shrieked as she bodysurfed in to shore.

▶ **Read Matthew 4:1–11. What wrong things was Jesus tempted to do?**

God doesn't command Christians to sit by themselves on the beach building grand sandcastles. The riotous fun is in the water—living life, playing, enjoying friends, working, studying, watching Christ walk on the water. It's where you get to chuckle, smile, and cheer.

Most waves are great fun.

But some are killers that knock down and drown people who play in them.

23

Evil is almost always a good thing out of control—a wave gone extreme, out of bounds, past God's plan. Evil is words (a good thing) twisted into a knife (a bad thing). Or a desire to fit with friends churned into a fear of your peers. It's self-esteem swollen into pride or selfishness. Or sex breaking the boundary of marriage. Or using the power of drugs to hurt rather than heal.

Jesus was pounded by waves gone twisted and gargantuan. He was tempted to meet a good need—hunger—at the wrong time, when God had told Him to pray. Jesus could have flung himself from the temple to show off God's care for Him, making a splash to gain followers. Or He could have accepted Satan's invitation to ride to kinghood of the world on a wave that bypassed the cross.

To each temptation Jesus said, "Good thing. But wrong time. Wrong way. No way." The waves didn't knock Him down because He pursued God's plan. He knew better than to try to ride killer waves.

Christians don't hide on the beach. Life is out in the waves. But they're smart enough to watch out for waves that want to pound them.

———————

Jesus said to him, "Away from me, Satan! For it is written: 'Worship the Lord your God, and serve him only.' "

MATTHEW 4:10

8

If You're So Smart

Laura grimaced at the poster Adrianne and Paul were making for their youth group's Christmas musical. To be honest, the head on Adrianne's shepherd looked as if it had been crushed in an accident, and Paul had run out of room writing the date, time, and place.

"Can you make it any uglier?" Laura sassed. "Are you *trying* to scare people away? Anyone who looks at that will think we're doofs. Of course, that does fit most of you anyway. We sound awful. Most of the cast can't act. You should hear our school musical. That's a real group, of course. We had tryouts and Mr. Malone said I was the directors' first choice. We didn't take just anyone, of course."

"Of course," Paul mimicked. "Anything else, O great one?"

"You don't have to get mad or anything. I just don't want anyone to think that this musical is all the better I can do."

✔ **Read James 3:13–18. What's the difference between real brains and fake brains?**

Imagine a relay race with millions of runners on the track at one time, each caught up in catching and passing on a gigantic baton. Runners can enter the race at any time. Here's the really bizarre part: No one races against anyone else. The goal is to get everyone to the finish line in good time.

That's what being a believer is like. We're all in the race. We work together. James says that if you have real brains you help others along in the race. You do good with humility, deliberately accepting people who are less mature, skilled, or smart than you. You don't just look out for yourself. You show gentleness not because you're weak, but because you're strong.

When you have fake brains, on the other hand, you rush to defeat others. You cheat. You loosen other runners' cleats. You wallop people and trip them midstride to get to the front of the pack.

James says not to pretend you're trying to do good. You're just trying to look good.

Who is wise and understanding among you? Let him show it by his good life, by deeds done in the humility that comes from wisdom.

JAMES 3:13

9

Tummy Toaster

"My feet are really cold!" Drew shouted to friends ahead on the trail. They kept skiing. "I mean it!"

"Whiner!" one yelled back.

A half hour later everyone rested at a fork in the trail.

"Drew—I hear your feet are cold," said Jeff, their trail guide. "Slip a boot off."

"No, they're okay. Really. I'm fine." Drew didn't want to be a whiner.

"I want to see your feet," Jeff insisted. He looked at Drew's right foot, then yanked up his own jacket and shirt. He knelt down and put Drew's icy foot on his bare stomach.

"Yike!" one of the girls yipped. "That has to feel good."

While Jeff thawed Drew's left foot he talked to the group. "Why didn't you stop earlier?" he wanted to know. "Drew's feet are frostbitten. We'll have to cut our day short and ski with Drew back to the lodge."

📭 **Read 2 Timothy 2:19–22. Why do you need Christian friends?**

You show weakness, and a friend calls you a baby. You share a secret with someone you trust, and two hours later you read it scrawled on a bathroom stall. You ask for help, and forevermore you're treated like an idiot. It's as if you dialed *9–1–1* and no one answered.

Big deal, you say. You can live without friends.

Wrong. You can't. At least not without the right kind of friends.

Deciding you want to chase hard after God—that you want to flee evil, do right, trust God, and love others—won't work unless you follow the rest of Paul's advice: Run alongside others who are running toward God.

Christians are the only ones going the same direction you are, pressing toward the same goal. It's possible that even real Christians—the ones who chase after God with all their hearts—may ice you sometimes. But if they've truly been warmed by God, they can't help sharing that warmth with you (Philippians 2:1–4). People who are continually cold don't know God (1 John 4:7–8).

You need help from other Christians. Take it. You can't thaw your own feet.

Flee the evil desires of youth, and pursue righteousness, faith, love and peace, along with those who call on the Lord out of a pure heart.

2 TIMOTHY 2:22

10

Not Snots

Heather switched to Oakbrook Middle School in December, and because she was a new student the school rules allowed her to try out late for whatever group or team she wanted. The cheerleading squad didn't exactly cheer when she picked their group. After Heather did some routines from her last school, the squad told her they needed to meet alone.

"I think we should let Heather in," Jennifer suggested. "Have you seen her older brother? He's cute."

"I like our group the way it is," Trish announced. "There's no way she can learn our routines midyear. I think we should tell her to . . ."

"Pop the big head, Trish," Stacy interrupted. "Our routines aren't that hard. We don't have any reason to leave anyone out. Admit it. You just don't like Heather."

In the end, the team voted "no" on Heather.

Part of us thinks *So what? Too bad so sad.* Heather won't spend life sleeping in a gutter because brats bashed her self-esteem. *Everyone gets left out sometimes, right?*

Another part of us knows it's not right to leave Heather out.

But just because a rule tells us to be nice to someone doesn't mean we will.

Read Matthew 28:16–20. In some of His last few words on earth, what does Jesus say to His followers?

What Jesus gives us as believers isn't just for us. He welcomes us into a friendship with himself. He wants us to welcome others into the same friendship. We can't act like the captains of a snotty squad, picking who to let in and who to shut out.

It's awful to leave someone off a team. It's beyond awful when we allow our nastiness—the tiniest bit of "Tough luck. I don't like you. I don't care about you"—to shut him or her out of friendship with God and His people, now and forever. Bad stuff.

When Jesus gathered His followers (His "disciples," people learning from Him) to speak to them, most worshiped Him—they fell on the ground in awe. Some others doubted. Their faith in Him was immature. Yet Jesus said the same thing to all of them: "I am Master of All. Go invite others to join the race. I'll go with you."

Therefore go and make disciples of all nations. . . .

MATTHEW 28:19

11

Shortcut to Disaster

On his thirteenth birthday Marc's parents gave him the keys to a rebuilt classic Mustang. It was his ticket to immediate and total coolness. Sure, it had to sit in the garage for three years until he got his driver's license, but how many other thirteen-year-olds owned a car?

Not that it was easy to wait to drive. Sometimes when his parents were gone Marc backed the car out on the driveway. When that became a bore he drove the car around the neighborhood. The risk made it exciting—state law said he would wait until eighteen to get a license if he was caught driving underage.

By the time Marc graduated from high school his Mustang was as hot as ever and he had indeed attained coolness. He had the right car, the right friends, the right looks.

He wasn't around to enjoy it for long. Just after graduation he died in an accident.

Read Psalm 73. (It's a little long but definitely worth the read.) How do you feel when others seem to have it made?

Some people get all the good stuff sooner than you do. A few get it by working hard and doing what's right.

But lots of others get it by taking shortcuts: They talk behind people's backs and win friends. They impress others with their stuff, not with who they are. They give away their body to get a boyfriend or girlfriend. They're cool. They know it. Everyone knows it.

When everything goes right for them, you feel jealous. You want what they've got, and want it yesterday. You think, *Why can't that be me?* You wonder if you've been wasting your time following God. You start to plot shortcuts you could take.

It's easy to feel like that until you realize one thing: Success gained by doing wrong won't last long. God promises that people who do wrong will lose control and crack up, like a driver who skids off a cliff. One moment the cool ones cruise. The next moment they crash.

Having everything doesn't mean you have it made. Having it made is enjoying God—and enjoying what He gives you, when and how He chooses (1 Timothy 6:6).

Those who are far from you will perish; you destroy all who are unfaithful to you. But as for me, it is good to be near God. I have made the Sovereign LORD my refuge. . . .

PSALM 73:27–28A

12
Bowser

Standing on a little hill across the street from school, Kim puffed a cigarette as Bus 93 pulled by. *Losers. They're all staring at me. I know it. I hope they like what they see.* Kim never took the bus with the kids from her neighborhood anymore. She walked early to hang with friends on the hill.

In elementary school kids called her "Crybaby Kimberly" because she wailed when nailed in dodgeball. And in middle school the boys twisted her last name, Bowers, into the nickname "Bowser"—as in *woof, woof, doggie.* Kids picked on her because she always knew the answers, always finished on time, always did what she was supposed to do.

One day she decided she was tired of being a goody-goody. Kimberly the Pastel Priss transformed herself into Kim the chain-smoking, pot-puffing, attitude-spewing Makeup Monster.

📝 **Read Galatians 6:7–10. What do you do when you're sick of being good?**

You don't know if you can hold out any longer. *I should get detention so I fit in better. If I do too well I'll get called a "brain." If I laugh at their jokes they'll like me. If I answer teachers' questions kids will think I'm a kiss-up.* So you give up and give in.

But being bad and being a goody-goody aren't your only options. You can choose to be good God's way.

You're a goody-goody if you remind people how good you are. Or if you do good to make others look bad. Or if you live to keep rules instead of keeping rules to live.

Being good God's way is an altered attitude and approach. You choose God's way because you trust that sooner or later it leads to life. You do what's right quietly and steadily because you believe God's promise that good behavior has good results.

God doesn't command you to do good to wreck life, but to give life. Being bad is tossing your life away. Being a goody-goody is asking to be boring and friendless. Being good—being obedient God's way—is getting set for God's best.

Let us not become weary in doing good,
for at the proper time we will reap a harvest
if we do not give up.

GALATIANS 6:9

PART 2

Finding your

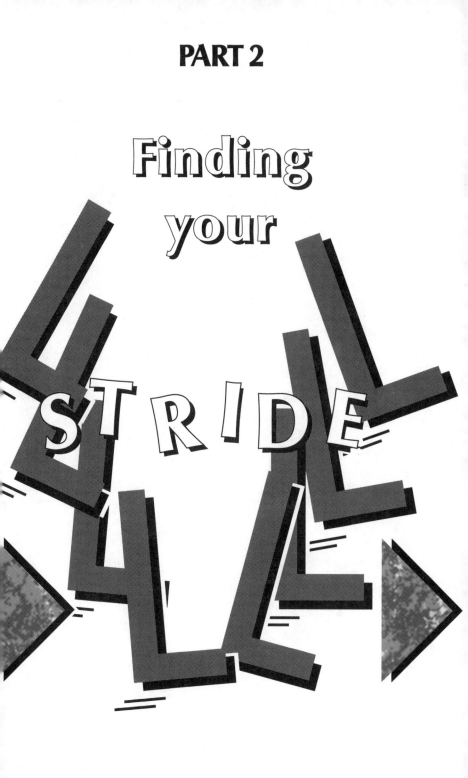

STRIDE

13
Just Do It
Doesn't Do It

Derek and his dad returned from their hunting trip with a ten-point buck roped to the roof of their mini-van. "It should have been Derek's," his dad told everyone when he bragged how they got the deer.

Derek faked a smile. He knew he should feel disappointed, but he wasn't sure he was.

He didn't know what he felt. Sitting in a tree stand with his dad waiting for deer, Derek pretended to be happy. When a deer finally wandered by, he wasn't sure he could kill it. He had never seen a deer so close, except for the stuffed head mounted above his grandparents' fireplace. But Dad had promised him the first shot, and Derek didn't want to disappoint him.

"Shoot! Just shoot!" his dad hissed. The buck's ears perked and Derek paused a second more, then finally pulled the trigger. All he hit was ground. When the buck bolted his dad quickly shot. Dad didn't miss.

🖊 **Read Jeremiah 1:4–10. How did Jeremiah react to God's expectations of him?**

When you fail—or you're scared you will—you try to shrug it off or make excuses or say it doesn't matter. But in the back of your brain the truth rattles around: You want to do well. So you're bugged. You're embarrassed. And you probably wouldn't admit your lack of perfection even to God without checking who's listening.

When God made Jeremiah a prophet (someone who would speak to God's people, the nation of Israel) Jeremiah was scared. God sent Jeremiah to go nose to nose with kings and leaders and the whole nation.

Jeremiah didn't think God's expectations fit him: "God, you're way off. I'm too young. I can't speak."

But God's expectations always fit us. He knows us. He knows how He made us. He sees more in us than we see in ourselves. And He knows He can make us able to do what He asks.

God let Jeremiah doubt for a second. Then God said, "Don't worry about it. *I* will send you. *I* will be with you. *I* will make you strong." He doesn't bark "Just do it" or "Just shoot it." He works patiently with us until we get to His goal.

But the LORD said to me, "Do not say, 'I am only a child.' You must go to everyone I send you to and say whatever I command. Do not be afraid of them, for I am with you and will rescue you," declares the LORD.

JEREMIAH 1:7–8

14
A Real No-Brainer

You watch your brain float overhead as you lie on an examination table. Your brain jumps and wriggles as lasers shoot from the walls to probe it.

"Basically empty, compared to ours," a space alien doctor says to his colleagues. *Great. They must have figured out that I flunked my last math test. My parents don't even know that.* As they tuck your brain painlessly back into your head they scan the rest of your body. *I can't wait to hear the results of this one.*

"Muscular structure: Unremarkable. Molecular composition: Mostly water. Chemical value of creature in earth money: Six dollars and two cents."

"Note the bad haircut," another doctor interjects.

"Yes, of course. I think we all agree with my recommendation: Vaporize."

✔ **Read Colossians 3:5–14. What do you want people to notice when they look at you?**

When God made us, He planned that people would see *Him* when they saw us. Unfortunately, sin has deformed our features so that we no longer look like God.

Quiz time: If you gave God, who is utterly perfect, the chance to make you look like Him again, which of the following would best describe you? (a) The wardrobe and plastic good looks of Ken or Barbie; (b) The musical talents of the Beach Boys; (c) The brains of Einstein; (d) The vertical jump of Michael Jordan; or (e) None of the above.

In heaven we will receive a new body that may or may not include choices *a*, *b*, *c*, and *d* above. But for now, God's first concern is something else: He wants to remake your *character* so that you think, feel, speak, and act like Him.

The "old self" is human nature deformed. It's all the things that make you ugly, unlike God. God says to get rid of those things completely—put them to death. The "new self" is just the opposite. It looks more like God each day. Those are the things God sculpts in you when you let Him. He remakes you to look like Him.

People should notice more than brains, looks, or talent when they probe your life. They should see a new you who looks like God.

Therefore, as God's chosen people, holy and dearly loved, clothe yourselves with compassion, kindness, humility, gentleness and patience.

COLOSSIANS 3:12

15
Don't Look Now

9:00 A.M. Your principal announces over the school's intercom that your *Save the Ducklings* poster won first prize from the state Animal Humane Society.

9:02 A.M. Your social studies teacher sends you to chat with the principal about the celebration dance you did on your desk.

10:00 A.M. Between classes your best friend thanks you for helping her study for a math test.

10:02 A.M. Your significant other dumps you like yesterday's trash.

12:00 noon. Sitting in a lunch-hour detention for your desk disco you receive an after-school detention for passing notes.

3:00 P.M. You ponder why half the world loves you and half the world thinks you're a mutant gnat. Which is it?

☑ **Read Psalm 19:7–14. How do you figure out what you're really like?**

Imagine what might happen if you blew your nose and missed the tissue, sliming your collar. Your own eyes can't quite twist to spot your problem. Some people point, laugh, and walk away. Others suppose you already know and don't want to interfere with your

41

right to accessorize however you want. Still others might call you a trendsetter. Only a real friend would whisper in your ear and send you scrambling for a mirror.

You could walk around looking stupid for a long time.

All of us have flaws we can't see. Yet the evaluations of others aren't always accurate. Their criticisms can be too harsh, or their support too kind. They may not know right from wrong. Even our own consciences can goof (1 Corinthians 4:4).

What others think does matter. God expects us to heed authorities like teachers and police (Romans 13:1). He wants us to obey our parents (Colossians 3:20). God puts other Christians around us to "speak the truth in love," to correct us (Ephesians 4:15).

But above all else, we listen to God's opinion of us. We aren't wackos who think we have a satellite link to God. We simply hear God speak in the Bible, teaching us right from wrong through His "laws," "statutes," "precepts," and "commands." We listen to Him because we know His opinion is more important than anyone else's, and what He says isn't meant to hurt us. He speaks out of love, to help us.

He's definitely the kind of friend who whispers in your ear.

———————

The law of the LORD is perfect, reviving the soul. The statutes of the LORD are trustworthy, making wise the simple. . . . Who can discern his errors? Forgive my hidden faults.

PSALM 19:7, 12

16

At Our Ugliest

Mitch Stetson became quarterback when his coach discovered Mitch didn't need an offensive line. He was three years ahead of his time, so much bigger and better than the other boys in his grade that he could fend off opponents with one hand while he bulleted rib-busting passes with the other.

Mitch was the most popular person in school. Boys imitated the way he combed his hair at the restroom mirror. Girls gawked when he walked, spinning around quickly when he looked their way so he wouldn't catch them staring.

Then he got zits.

His face erupted into a million red, oozing volcanoes. Girls turned away to avoid gagging at Lavaface. Boys found other friends. Coach replaced Mitch with someone bigger and better. And one day Mitch stopped looking in mirrors. Even he couldn't stand to look at himself.

📖 **Read Romans 5:6–8. What can you do to make God look away and stop loving you?**

Sometimes you feel like you have a zit the size of a golf ball smack in the middle of your forehead, like a third eye. It's big. It's ugly. It's a flaw that makes you feel unlovable.

You might think you're stupid. You might hate how you look. Your flaw might be something you've done wrong, or an embarrassing family situation. It might be a dark secret you hardly admit to yourself.

You might try to hide your faults from yourself, your friends, and your family. You can't hide anything from God. He sees everything. And He still likes you.

He proved it. Not many people would die for a religious snob ("righteous" in Romans 5:7 probably means someone with right actions but a cold heart). A few people might give their life to save a good person, or a friend. No one would think of dying for a reject, a flawed, sinful person, but God did. He proved His love for us by sending Christ to die for us not when we were perfect, but at "just the right time," when we were at our worst.

God doesn't look away. Ever.

But God demonstrates his own love for us in this: While we were still sinners, Christ died for us.

ROMANS 5:8

44

17

Starting Over

"It's not like I'm a murderer or anything," Keri told the girls in her Bible study. "But I have a potty mouth. I can talk pretty while I'm around my Christian friends, but other than that I swear all the time. If my little brother hits me, I swear. If a teacher does something I don't like, I cuss under my breath. It's a bad habit.

"But the real problem is I feel bad all the time about it. I know it's wrong to sin, so I imagine God glaring at me and giving me the silent treatment. I wonder if I'm going to hell. All Christianity does for me is make me feel like a failure. I don't want that."

Read John 7:53—8:11. What helped the woman caught sinning start over?

Sometimes we're legends in our own minds. We think we're perfect. We might be rotten people who never feel guilt, or like the Pharisees in the Bible—nice church people who don't smoke, drink, or swear, but ooze pride, anger, and selfishness.

At other times we admit we sin. But our honest guilt turns into fear that we never do anything right, and that God won't forgive us when we blow it.

Jesus deals with the woman's sin matter-of-factly, like a doctor who says, "Yep, you're sick. But we can deal with that." Jesus doesn't hide her sin. The woman was caught sleeping with someone's husband. He didn't say she didn't deserve death, the punishment Jewish law prescribed. But He set her free. He says simply, "I do not condemn you. . . . Leave your life of sin."

God treats us the same way: He expects us to admit our wrongdoing, because we all sin. But if we admit our sins to God He promises to forgive us, washing away our guilt and putting our friendship with Him back on track (1 John 1:8–9).

That's what gives us the freedom to start over. And over. And over if we need to.

Christians aren't perfect. Unlike cows and horses, we can't run as soon as we get out of the womb. Like little babies, at first we lie helpless. Then we flip, roll, scoot, crawl, and stand. Muscles and balance develop. *Then* we walk.

But we never walk—or run—without getting up from the pavement a lot.

Go now and leave your life of sin.

JOHN 8:11

18
Good for Something

By the middle of seventh grade Ben was treading in deep water and gasping for breath. His grades were dismal. He was booted off the soccer team when he tripped and sprained his toe in the season opener—and broke the leg of the team's star center. His boss at the nursing home where he volunteered told him he annoyed the residents. Teachers politely informed him he couldn't sing, act, or draw, and that he should try to find himself somewhere else. Then he signed up for a Chinese class at a community center and found out "Ben" sounds like "stupid" in Mandarin.

"Everyone's good at something, dear," his mom cooed. "You'll find something."

"Quit it, Mom!" Ben moaned. "You're my mother. You have to like me. But I'm not good at anything."

At times everyone feels like a child only a mother could love.

🖋 **Read Romans 12:1–8. How do you find out what you're good at?**

Sometimes mothers are right. "Don't worry, dear. You'll find *something* you're good at"—these aren't just nice words from Mom. The Bible says the same thing: God gives everyone gifts. But how do you find yours?

Get the big picture. The Bible lists loads of gifts—here in Romans 12, in 1 Corinthians 12:7–11, and Ephesians 4:11–13. And those lists are only examples.

Don't expect applause. Some gifts put you up front where people *ooh* and *aah.* People seldom clap if you're kind, giving, encouraging, or even good at leading or serving. Just because no one says "Wow!" doesn't mean you bombed.

Try it out. God gives gifts to build up Christians. Offer to help at church. You don't figure out what you're good at sitting around, or by trying something only once.

Be yourself. Even Christians can rip on people with different gifts. Sometimes you'll feel odd even when you're doing the right thing (1 Corinthians 12:14–26).

You begin to find your gifts, though, when you *make yourself available to God.* For starters, that's the only right response to everything God gives us. And as you follow Him you'll find your way.

Just as each of us has one body with many members, and these members do not all have the same function, so in Christ we who are many form one body, and each member belongs to all the others. We have different gifts. . . .

ROMANS 12:4–6A

19

No One Cried Foul

You worked so hard.

You got nothing for it.

Last year your entry in the 4-H amphibian fair—Bob the ninja turtle—didn't even place. This year your Lolita wowed the judges with her swamp-green nail polish, lipstick, and tail bow, as well as the fake eyebrows you penciled on Lolita to make her look like your aunt Beverly. And spectators loved Lolita's snappy turtle wax coat, which you had buffed to a fine shine in shop. Yet when you and Lolita took the stand to bask in the admiration of fellow hobbyists, another contestant snuck in, charged the medal stand, hipchecked you out of the way, and claimed Lolita and your prize for himself.

No one noticed. No one cried "Foul! Impostor! Unfair!"

Ripoff.

Read Hebrews 6:7–12. Is it worth working hard when hard work doesn't always win the prize?

Every action has two audiences.

Fans on earth are fickle. They seldom know when to clap. You study for an exam until your brain bursts, but a classmate who swipes the answer key gets the highest grade. You play tough all season long, yet the

49

coach plays favorites when he gives the MVP award. Or you leave a party early to get home by curfew and peers jeer.

Fans on earth even clap for people who deserve to be booed to bits.

But your Fan in heaven is faithful. God always spots a job well done. He sees when you do something "spiritual" like praying or reading your Bible. But He notices *all* the ways you obey Him—when you do homework and chores, listen to your parents, play hard, respect teachers, treat people great.

When you dedicate yourself to doing good you're like a patch of soil that soaks up rain and grows a bumper crop for its master. God won't forget that. Trust Him. Be patient and you'll enjoy the harvest.

———————

God is not unjust; he will not forget your work and the love you have shown him as you have helped his people and continue to help them.

HEBREWS 6:10

20
Faster, Higher, Stronger

Monique anxiously awaited her turn at her first all-district gymnastics meet. *There are so many people watching*, she thought. Monique did fine in her first two events, but in the floor exercise she missed a landing and bounced out of bounds, which dropped her score to the bottom few of all the girls competing. She ran back to her teammates crying, furious with herself.

Her coach tried to encourage her. "Monique, you did great. We'll work on landings and some endurance training and next time you'll . . ."

"I'm not going to do this anymore," she snapped. "I'm not any good at gymnastics. I made a fool of myself."

Read Hebrews 12:4–11. If God loves you, why does He let you struggle?

You didn't stop toddling when you banged your face on the furniture a few times, and you kept trying at math even though $2+2=4$ bewildered you. And no doubt you'll do whatever it takes to keep growing up—to get your driver's license, rent your first apartment, and build a career and family.

Life is hard. Just because something takes effort doesn't mean you're stupid or lazy or uncoordinated or unspiritual. It means God is working on you.

God uses your struggles with school, home, sports, lessons, and relationships to discipline you—to *train* you—to make you strong, tough, and more like Him. That's not necessarily because you've been bad, but because He knows you can be better. God probably won't shoot lightning at your legs so you effortlessly win gymnastics meets. Nor does He zap your heart so you flawlessly obey Him.

You practice to get good at anything. You need to practice to master life, and to become a strong Christian.

God doesn't put you into training because He's a cruel coach who laughs while you run laps. He knows what it takes to make you mature—when to go easy and when to push hard, and His discipline is always perfectly planned for your good.

Discipline hurts. But it works.

No discipline seems pleasant at the time, but painful. Later on, however, it produces a harvest of righteousness and peace for those who have been trained by it.

HEBREWS 12:11

21
Mow Me Down

When Jason's older brother went off to college he arranged for Jason to take over his lawnmowing business. All Jason had to do was finish the last month and a half of fall mowing, then start the business up again next spring. He could make three times as much per hour than any of his friends. He would be rolling in green stuff.

But he had to mow it before he could roll in it. After spending a whole Saturday mowing—and not finishing what he needed to do—he recalled that his brother was a foot taller and sixty pounds bigger. And it took him five years to build his business.

This was more work than Jason had figured.

His mom felt sorry for him. His dad said he couldn't quit.

Jason whined that this experience was going to ruin his attitude toward work and threatened to live at home until he was forty.

☑ **Read James 1:2–5. If you're supposed to persevere ("stick with" stuff), when is it okay to quit?**

Your swim coach expects you at practice three hours a night, five nights a week. You're spending afternoons squished on a piano bench with the lady teaching you to play hits from *The Sound of Music*. Your dance instructor yells too much. And you just aren't any good at track.

Quitting a team or an activity or a job doesn't always mean you're a quitter. You need to quit when you're hurting yourself—when you can't get enough sleep, cry your eyes out nightly, or don't get your homework done. You don't have much choice but to quit when you're forced to do wrong—by a crooked boss, for example. And it's okay to quit when you can do better at something else, *after* you've stuck it out and kept your promises. Commitments you made first—not the ones you like best—come first. Get help while you sweat it out, even if that means someone else takes some of your jobs.

Bad times force you to rely on God. From the frontside trials are terrifying. From the backside you can see how God cared for you. But hanging in through the middle of a trial doesn't mean you have to sit back and let circumstances wallop you.

Consider it pure joy, my brothers, whenever you face trials of many kinds, because you know that the testing of your faith develops perseverance.

JAMES 1:2–3

22
Don't Play Dead

Part of Mort's job working the late shift at the funeral home was to whisk the ashes of cremated customers into brass urns. The job didn't pay well, but it presented certain, shall we say, golden opportunities.

Night after night Mort picked though the ashes of the day's dearly departed for a treasure of enduring worth: gold. A filling here, a dental bridge there. Once in a while he struck the mother lode—a shiny mouthful from an older lady or gentleman who had for decades successfully resisted being fitted with dentures. In time Mort accumulated enough extra income to retire early—on beachfront property in Rio at age thirty-five.

The best part was that his victims never fought back.

☑ Read Philippians 2:3–8. Does being a Christian mean you always play dead—and get torched—and let someone steal your fillings?

As Christians there is no better way to show love to others than to "lay down our lives" (1 John 3:16) by giving our time or our stuff sacrificially, by showing kindness to an enemy, by putting others before ourselves.

But we have only so much to give. So we give wisely.

If you left your school locker open with a sign on it saying "Look here! Steal my stuff!" you would foolishly have nothing left either for yourself or to share with people who really need it. If you let people take advantage of you then you won't be able to give when it really matters.

Christ gave because He was strong, not because He was weak.

No one walked all over Him. No one stole anything from Him. He *chose* to give, in both life and death: He "made himself nothing." He "humbled himself." Here's a strange one: Even when He was about to be taken by force to be beaten and crucified, He made it clear to his killers that He was dying by choice (Matthew 26:53–54).

Being robbed and giving a gift have the same result. You pay a price. But when you give by choice, people don't see a fool. They see Christ.

Your attitude should be the same as that of Christ Jesus: Who, being in very nature God, did not consider equality with God something to be grasped, but made himself nothing, taking the very nature of a servant. . . .

PHILIPPIANS 2:5–7

23
Fighting Forward

Tragedy struck today in northwest Wisconsin, the newscaster announced. *A Polk County deputy sheriff was critically wounded after he responded to a call for help in capturing a man sought for a shooting in Minnesota last night. Deputy Mike Seversen was shot under the chin at close range as he attempted to . . .*

Three days later Mike woke up in a hospital bed.

He couldn't move.

But he was alive.

📖 **Read Philippians 4:12–13. What's the toughest situation you could face without shattering?**

You probably don't think life ends when the air conditioning breaks or your VCR goes on strike. You probably don't doubt God's care for you when you blow a test or you can't afford $200 tennis shoes.

But what if you were paralyzed from the neck down? What if you couldn't walk, talk, or breathe on your own? Or if your brain biffed? Life is over when you hurt that bad, isn't it? Then it's time to give up on God and life, right?

Wrong.

Mike still can't use his arms or legs. He knows what he's lost. He's no fool.

But he also knows what he still possesses. He has God. He fought to learn to breathe and talk again. His brain works well. He hunts, works on his house, jokes with his family and friends. He teaches people about God's care.

Paul, like Mike, realized he could thrive with a less-than-perfect life. He was tougher than he knew. God was bigger than he thought. From prison Paul wrote that he could be happy in any circumstance, with little or plenty, because God made him strong.

You probably won't be shot trying to capture a criminal. But you won't escape bad times (John 16:32). Your life isn't finished when it falls apart—when the race turns into an uphill battle against the wind, with flies in your eyes and gnats in your nose. That isn't time to quit. It's time to see how tough God can make you.

I can do everything through him who gives me strength.

PHILIPPIANS 4:13

PART 3

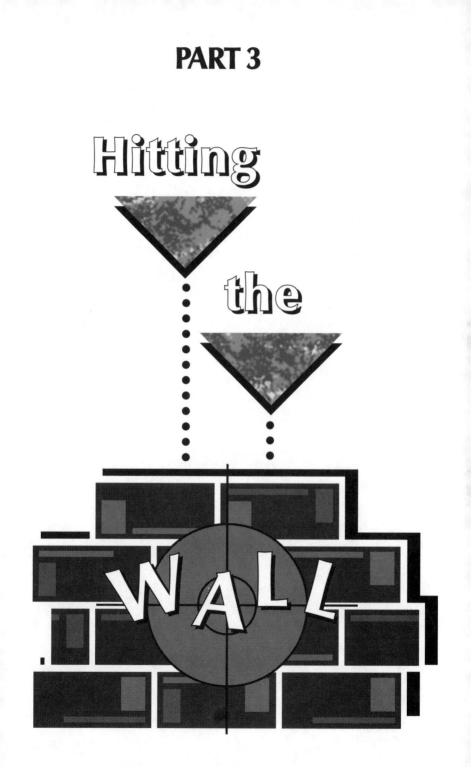

Hitting the WALL

24
Dream Vacation

The pictures in the tour brochure looked so pretty. Pictures lie.

Of course not everything about your family's vacation was awful. For starters, your bargain flight took off on time—at 2:38 A.M. And they did serve a meal in flight. Well, more of a snack. It looked like the pilot's leftovers from the airport lounge. Your rental car from Bob's Borrow-A-Bomb was good protection from carjackings. Your family was in no danger of looking like wealthy tourists. And your dad did earn one thumb up for trying to find a room in a different hotel.

But he got two thumbs down for making the reservation in the first place. Your mom had to clean the hotel bathtub before you could use it, and all week you slept on top of the bedcovers—to avoid infectious diseases. And on the one day nice enough to go to the beach the only place left to lay your towel was downwind from the porta-potties.

All week long a question whined in your mind: *Why is this happening to me?*

📝 **Read Psalm 22:1–11. Do believers ever wonder if God is worth trusting when things go wrong?**

Deep down we expect first-class accommodations on our journey as Christians—posh hotels, fast cars, and discount tickets to all the big attractions. We trust our all-knowing, all-perfect God to make the weather sunny and lines short.

When things go wrong, we feel cheated. It feels like our Father above booked us on a nightmarish trip with a fourth-class travel agency.

Psalm 22 shows how David wondered about God's travel plans for his life: *I've heard all sorts of stories, God, about how great you are. I've seen you myself. So where are you? Haven't you heard me? My enemies surround me. People think I'm crazy to trust you. I don't feel like I'm yours, yet I know that I've trusted you a long time. Please help soon!* Even the best of believers wonder where God is when trouble hits.

Yet sooner or later we figure it out: Our trip won't be perfect because the world we travel through is no paradise.

———————

My God, my God, why have you forsaken me? Why are you so far from saving me, so far from the words of my groaning?

PSALM 22:1

25
Whipped Potatoes

The food fight was well underway before Mrs. Heffermeister ambled toward the student cafeteria to do duty as lunch supervisor. But when she entered the lunchroom the fight escalated into war in an instant. Mrs. Heffermeister became the room's sole target. From every direction mashed potatoes whizzed and whirled and pelted her from head to toe. Kids hated Mrs. Heffermeister. She could whip any boy in the school—and most of the male teachers. No one was about to leave when she bellowed, "ENOUGH!" and made everyone sit still until the principal came.

Chad was innocent, of course. He had eaten his ammunition before the fight broke out. No one paid attention, though, when he argued that he didn't deserve to stay after school with the rest of the lunchroom.

It didn't occur to him how many times he had flung food in the past without getting caught.

✔ **Read Psalm 36:1–9. Why is the world such a messy place?**

Are food fights funny? Sure. Are they right? No—for lots of reasons: the mess you expect someone else to clean up, the disrespect you show for authority, the food you waste while kids starve. So why are they funny?

Deep down we love to fling mashed potatoes.

It would probably be okay if we stopped there. But we do much worse. Human beings deceive, envy, tease, bash, and kill one another. We steal each other's dignity and let children go hungry. We think neglect and violence and divorce are normal.

God intended the world to be a place where we believe in Him enough to do right—not only because we fear His anger but because we trust His wisdom. We were meant to bask in His love, swim in His goodness, rest in the shade of His protection, feast at His beachside barbecue sloshing down cold colas. Life was to be a summer vacation.

But humanity (Romans 3:23) chooses to live in the lunchroom throwing food—scorning God, cooking up more ammunition, and high-fiving each other every time a target takes a hit. Christians have gotten free to see the sun, but from time to time even we go back inside to wallow in the mess.

We've spoiled paradise.

———————

Your love, O LORD, reaches to the heavens, your faithfulness to the skies. Your righteousness is like the mighty mountains, your justice like the great deep.

PSALM 36:5—6A

26

Quit Gawking and Do Something

Ooooooo. . . . Stars swirl as you lie on the floor. "He slipped on a banana peel on his way to Sunday school," you hear a friend say. "He hit his head pretty hard."

Your youth pastor pokes his face into yours. "God did this to you," he smirks. "It's because you put cereal in my sleeping bag on our last retreat."

"No, no, no. His parents are far too permissive," declares your third-grade Sunday school teacher. "I can't count the times I told him not to run with scissors."

"It's a hormone thing," mumbles a doctor. "He's at that awkward age."

An elder casts demons out of the banana peel. A parent scolds your youth pastor for his carelessness in teaching the church's youth. Finally a lawyer walks by and whispers in your ear. "It's the church's fault. Let's sue them for waxing the floor."

☑ **Read John 9:1–12. Who's to blame when bad things happen to people?**

Admit it. You're responsible for most of what happens in your life. You flipped the banana peel, then it flipped you. You cut class, so you flunked. You were lazy and got canned. You didn't hustle, so the other team scored.

Peers and parents and hormones influence you. But they don't make your choices. You do. And you live with the consequences of your choices.

At other times you're slugged by a situation you didn't choose. You catch the flu. Your parents divorce. You're beaten up or abused. You discover you're dyslexic.

You're not to blame, though you still control how you respond.

Jesus' disciples accepted popular opinion about the man born blind: Hardship hit because someone sinned. The only question was who had sinned—the man (before birth, they thought!) or his parents. Jesus rejected both explanations.

And He said the disciples missed the whole point: What was God going to do?

That's still the point. When bad things happen God wants to work through *us*—through our helpful actions. He can move through the *miraculous*—out-of-the-ordinary displays of His power. And He's even glorified through the *tenacious*—people who rely on His strength to whip bad situations that don't go away.

In Jesus' eyes the blind man wasn't a puzzle to solve. He was a person to help.

"Neither this man nor his parents sinned," said Jesus, "but this happened so that the work of God might be displayed in his life. As long as it is day, we must do the work of him who sent me."

JOHN 9:3–4

27
Heart Attack

How could God let this happen? If God really loved Jim, Jodi thought, *he wouldn't be lying in a coma. If God really cared, He would have kept that truck from plowing into Jim's car in the first place.*

Jodi was sure God could work wonders to put her brother back together. She just didn't know if He would.

📖 **Read Acts 20:17–24, where the apostle Paul is saying goodbye to Ephesian church leaders. Is it right to expect God to do miracles?**

People have no shortage of agonizing problems—crunched friendships, twisted minds, exploding families, sick bodies. Yet while our outsides fall apart, an even deadlier problem hides inside: We don't know God well. Our hearts have stopped beating for Him.

Paul saw that God shaped all the experiences of his life, good and bad, miracles and failures, to address that one problem. God wanted, first of all, for Paul to know Him well, and then for others to know Him too. Paul focused his whole life on God's rescue plan—staying close to God and completing the job God gave him to do, following God even when he couldn't see ahead, even when it looked like God's plans led to pain. Being part of God's rescue squad was more important to Paul than any pain he suffered (2 Corinthians 6:3–12).

From God's perspective, our need for Him is the real emergency. God wants to jumpstart our hearts.

When we become friends with God through Christ, our hearts pump anew. When we help others become His friends as well, more hearts pump.

Our plan is for God to fix our circumstances.

God's plan is to fix us.

That doesn't mean God leaves us twisting in pain. When we pray we ask for what we believe is best—to have a brother back, for a friendship to heal, for parents to stick together. We act where we can and ask God to act where we can't. God does what He sees best to jumpstart hearts, and to accomplish all the other plans and purposes He has for us.

Sometimes God works unbelievable miracles for our outsides. When we let Him, He always works miracles on our insides.

———————

However, I consider my life worth nothing to me, if only I may finish the race and complete the task the Lord Jesus has given me—the task of testifying to the gospel of God's grace.

ACTS 20:24

28

Your Mother Wears Combat Boots

Billy was walking to school minding his own business when Bruce and company jumped him for his lunch money. Bruce sat on Billy's chest and knuckled his forehead to make him whimper before really punishing him.

Suddenly a screech from the end of the block distracts Bruce. One of Bruce's lookouts yells, "Mother on a rampage! RUN!"

They stumble over each other trying to escape as Billy's mother steams toward them in fatigues, face paint, and whomping black boots. She heaves the bullies over fences into their own backyards, but not before threatening to push their noses into the back of their brains the next time they touch Billy.

Billy gets up. "Thanks, Mom."

"No problem," says Billy's mom. "Anything for my cutesy-wutesy baby."

✔ **Read Psalm 144:1–8. Does needing God's help make you a wimp?**

You would probably rather go home with a black eye than be rescued by your mother. But some battles you can't fight yourself.

Even David—the fierce warrior who wrote Psalm

144—admitted he needed God. Without God he was nothing—a "breath," a "fleeting shadow." He begged God not to stand by. He asked God to split the sky, toast the mountains, and shoot lightning at His enemies. David needed God to rescue him.

That doesn't mean believers are weak. God does dash down the block and toss enemies over fences. But He also arms you to defend yourself.

Because David was king of Israel, a political country ruled by God, he saw his enemies as foreign nations who served other gods. *Your* biggest enemies aren't people. They're spiritual. And they don't want your lunch money. They want to bully you out of your faith. God gives you weapons to strike back: truth, righteousness, the good news of Christ, faith, prayer, sureness that you belong to God, and the Bible (Ephesians 6:10–18). God's weapons all defend and strengthen your trust in God.

Needing God doesn't make you a baby. You never grow out of your need for Him.

He is my loving God and my fortress, my stronghold and my deliverer, my shield, in whom I take refuge, who subdues peoples under me.

PSALM 144:2

29

Next Time I'll Floss

Gzzzzzzzzer goes the drill into the surface of your tooth. You flinch. "Does that hurt?" your dentist inquires.

Hurt? Would it hurt if I twisted my finger in your eye at 6000 rpm?

"Just a little," you respond politely. "Maybe I need another shot." When three shots of novocaine do nothing for your agony, you stop contemplating how much money you'll get for pain and suffering when you sue your dentist. You start wishing you had paid more attention to your mom's accounts of pain-in-childbirth. *How did she breathe? Hoo-hoo-hee?*

Your bleary mind makes a deal with the dentist. *Stop it! Stop it! Next time I'll floss!*

Your dentist pauses—to let the filling dry, he says as he heads out the door. *So why does he keep bobbing in to check on me? To see if I'm dead?*

📖 **Read Isaiah 40:27–31. How do you know God hears you when you pray for help?**

You would settle for less than a miracle. You just want a little something to take the edge off your pain. And you wonder why God doesn't respond to your generous offer to become a missionary to Ukarumpa in exchange for a little help now.

But nothing happens. You think God has said, "Forget it, slimeball. Chew dirt!" and you get aggravated.

Hello, God! Can't you see I'm hurting? Quit ignoring me. Why won't you answer me?

He has.

God doesn't sleep or go to lunch. And He doesn't put a price on His services. He doesn't hear you because of *your* promises to Him but because of *His* promise to you: You belong to Him. He sees your problems and hears your prayers.

But He answers prayers the way He knows is best (1 John 5:14–15).

He doesn't always say "Yes." But He's not necessarily saying "No." Sometimes He says "Wait" or "I'll answer, but not the way you think." When you trust God He renews your strength—to walk, to run, to fly. Or to defy life's drills.

———————

. . . but those who hope in the LORD will renew their strength. They will soar on wings like eagles; they will run and not grow weary, they will walk and not be faint.

ISAIAH 40:31

72

30
Out of Cash

Colleen's mom sat at the kitchen table with her checkbook and a stack of bills. After each bill she carefully figured how much money was left.

"I'm sorry, honey," she told Colleen when she got to the bottom of the pile. "There's not much left. Enough for a pair of pants when school starts, and a shirt at the end of next month."

Only one pair of pants? Colleen thought. It was a good thing her mom hadn't noticed the hole in the bottom of Colleen's shoes, or she would be getting shoes instead of pants. Colleen knew she could hide the hole from the kids at school—at least until it rained and her feet got wet and stunk. She couldn't hide old worn clothes.

Colleen knew that her mom was doing her best to provide for the family, but she still felt sick. *I'm going to look like a troll—like I crawled out from under a bridge. I'll be the only one not wearing new stuff!*

Read Isaiah 43:1–4. Where is God when you suffer?

When you struggle through deep waters it's normal for questions to pour in: Why won't God fix my problem *now*? When will God punish the people who hurt me?

Why do bad things happen to me? Where is God when I hurt?

When you ache you feel like a reject. You're sure you're the only one who botched the test. You assume you're the only one whose parents fight or work too much. You glance in the mirror on your way out the door and you convince yourself that you're the only one whose clothes are less than wonderful, or whose bangs wanged.

When you suffer you feel like you're alone.

You're not.

When God doesn't jam His hand into your life and immediately fix your problems you might think He's left you to fend for yourself. He hasn't. You belong to him. He "redeemed" you in Christ, paid the price to make you His child (Colossians 1:13–14). And He's smack in the middle of your problem with you. He feels what you go through. And He makes sure that even if you fight the flood and feel the heat, you won't be overwhelmed.

"Fear not, for I have redeemed you; I have called you by name; you are mine. When you pass through the waters, I will be with you. . . ."

ISAIAH 43:1B–2A

31
Get Real

"You gotta get over it." Steven tried to knock sense into Tom. "I know what you're thinking—that you can get your parents back together and make everything the way it used to be. Forget it, Tom. Stuff won't ever be the same. I should know. It's been six years since my parents divorced. They treat me like a video rental. They borrow me for a few days and take me back when they've seen enough."

Steven didn't hold back what he thought about Tom's situation. "You learn to survive on your own. Hey—if you're smart you can take advantage of this whole thing. My dad tries to buy me because he knows Mom can't afford to keep up. I keep upping the price. I get something new every weekend. You'll make it if you just remember one thing. When they trash you, you trash them back."

Reality can be harsh.

☛ Read Romans 4:18–21. How did Abraham react to God's promise that he and his wife, Sarah—both way beyond baby-bearing age—would have a child?

Back at the beginning of the Bible, God told Abraham he would be the start of a great nation, God's chosen people. He couldn't father a nation without first fathering a family, and he and Sarah didn't have any kids. When Sarah heard God's promise, she laughed (Genesis 18:10–15). She thought, *Aren't you a little late, God?*

Abraham wasn't stupid. He knew as well as Sarah that their bodies were out of fire, ready to expire. He didn't ignore the problem. He faced facts. Yet he had faith. He was convinced that God would do what He had sworn to do.

Here's reality: Life hurts. Here's a bigger reality: God keeps promises.

These are the facts as you know them: You're starting at a new school and you're totally alone. But *God says He will never leave you* (Hebrews 13:5–6). These are the facts as you feel them: You want to tear off the eyebrows of people who hurt you. But *God promises to punish those who hurt you* (Romans 12:19). These are the facts as you see them day to day: Life at home or school is falling apart and you don't think you can cope. But *God promises to work through any difficulty to bring good to your life* (Romans 8:28).

What we see and feel can make God's promises sound crazy. But He always keeps His word.

[Abraham] did not waver through unbelief regarding the promise of God, but was strengthened in his faith and gave glory to God, being fully persuaded that God had power to do what he had promised.

ROMANS 4:20–21

32
God Is Angry Too

You and your dad were so delirious after watching your favorite team clinch a playoff spot that you determined post-game burger inhalation was the only way to wind down.

Halfway through your fast-food feeding frenzy two men with nylons over their heads burst into the restaurant waving shotguns. They herded everyone into the store freezer and made you lie on boxes of food with your hands behind your head. They jabbed your dad in the back with the shotgun and threatened to blow away anyone who moved.

A few minutes later their noise out front stopped. The men were gone.

But they aren't gone from your mind. When your best friend came over with a nylon stretched over his face you slammed the door and hid. Later that seemed funny. What isn't humorous is crying in the middle of the night, or shivering when you remember the freezer. And what makes you want to punch walls is that the men got away. You can't understand why God hasn't ~··t them on ice for good.

Read Habakkuk 3:3–16. When will God punish people who do wrong?

God is the one Being in the universe who is totally holy—totally powerful, wise, and good in everything He thinks, says, and does. He can't tolerate sin. Habakkuk's prayer recalls what God did to the Egyptians, Israel's slave masters, until Egypt finally let Israel go. Gory stuff.

God isn't just mad at Egyptians. He threatens eternal separation from himself and everything good for all who continue to fight Him. The Bible pictures the place of punishment for rebels (called "hell" in the Bible) as unstoppable fire (Revelation 21:8), everlasting chains (Jude 6), and utter darkness (Matthew 8:12). People who do evil will get what they deserve, even if they don't get caught on earth.

God is only ferociously angry with really bad people, right? Not *us*, right?

Compared to God, we're all really bad people. We all deserve separation from Him. But God doesn't wish hell on anyone (2 Peter 3:9). He waits for people to admit their sin, accept forgiveness, and live at peace with Him in heaven (Romans 6:23).

That's why He doesn't always ice enemies now. Sometimes God seems slow to punish people who sin. Be glad He wasn't quick to punish you.

———————

In wrath you strode through the earth and in anger you threshed the nations.

HABAKKUK 3:12

33

In the Meantime

Tasha and her pastor sat in the rec room of the hospital's mental health unit.

"They've got me locked up like I tried to kill some-one!" Tasha blurted.

"Tasha, you *did*. You tried to hurt Tasha. We won't let you do that."

"Well, this place is humiliating. They took away my shoelaces and my belt and my—you know. Anything they think I can use to hurt myself. I can't use the phone. You're the first person I've seen other than Mom. It's like jail." She quieted. "They did let me go for a supervised walk outside today. That was kind of nice. I haven't gone for a walk in a long time. Dad and I used to walk together. You never met him, did you?"

"He died before I moved here, remember? Tasha— your dad—is his death what this is about?"

Tasha started to cry. "I don't know—it's about my dad and my mom and my sister and my friends! I just wanted to get away."

✍ **Read Habakkuk 3:17–19. What do you do when hurts don't go away?**

You want to believe that God will help you through your problems. But you can't see Him, and you don't

79

always feel Him. What do you do when God seems slow to help?

You can choose to deal with your problem: Change what you can. Talk with people *who can find solutions*—parents, teachers, counselors, and pastors. Memorize Bible passages that encourage you.

You can choose to keep busy: Go out for a club. Exercise. Play sports. Goof with your friends. Do homework. Help around home. Find a hobby.

Most of all, you can choose to keep trusting God: When everything goes wrong (when "the fig tree doesn't bud" or "the fields produce no food") God is still Lord—He still watches over you. He's still Savior—He will rescue you. Sometimes God seems slow so we learn that even if all we have is Him, that's enough.

Those choices refresh, like plopping in front of a fan on a hot day.

Other choices are more like prying the protective cage off a fan and inserting your face. People who make those choices—to rebel, drink, inhale, misuse sex, hide in their rooms, weld headphones to their head, or quit life altogether—miss out on fingers and foreheads and noses. Or on life.

Though the fig tree does not bud and there are no grapes on the vines . . . yet I will rejoice in the Lord, I will be joyful in God my Savior.

HABAKKUK 3:17A—18

34

You Understand

Mrs. Bradley wanted Brian out. Out of her class. Out of her mind. Out of her life. He was a funny kid. But his defiance was catching on and destroying her class.

She had only one weapon left, one she saved for kids she hated: embarrassment. So with hopes of shaming Brian into behaving, she sent him across the street to the elementary school. For an hour a day for two weeks, Brian returned to second grade.

She thought it was punishment. Brian loved it. It got him out of her class.

From his big desk in the back of the room Brian noticed a little boy named Sam. He acted exactly like Brian—no focus, zippo attention span. Brian felt sorry for him.

One day Sam asked Brian for help, and Brian discovered he could explain the answer to Sam. When Sam's teacher tried to help Sam with his assignments, Brian realized how difficult he had made life for Mrs. Bradley.

Brian and Sam became study buddies. They understood each other.

Read 2 Corinthians 1:3–11. Can God make good come out of suffering?

The last thing you want to hear when you hurt is that your experience will make you stronger and wiser—as if that makes you glad to get dumped, or happy that a friend died, or excited to struggle with math.

But if you're honest you know that you do learn when bad things happen to you.

We're not exactly sure what Paul suffered in Asia. Whatever it was, Paul despaired intensely, scared as if he were shackled in an electric chair and someone was about to flip the switch. His experience shattered his confidence in himself. Yet he found that God was "the God of all comfort." And he shared that comfort with the Corinthians.

Rough times teach you what God knows you need to learn: Trust—a sureness that God accepts you, cares for you, and ultimately will bring you to an eternity with himself in paradise (Romans 5:3–4). You learn to rely on God, not on yourself.

God didn't plan for bad things to happen in your world. But like a piece of clay that's been squished out of shape, God can spin your life into something good again. He heals your hurt. And He uses you to heal the hurts of others. Your pain isn't a waste.

Praise be to the God and Father of our Lord Jesus Christ, the Father of compassion and the God of all comfort, who comforts us in all our troubles, so that we can comfort those in any trouble with the comfort we ourselves received from God.

2 CORINTHIANS 1:3–4

35
Waiting

Angela toweled off the steamy bathroom mirror so she could see to gently comb the few strands of hair left after her chemotherapy treatments. Her doctors had hoped the drugs had killed her cancer, but everyone had still sighed relief when she made it to her birthday.

Now as she got ready for her party she mulled whether to wear her wig or to go with the chic bald look her friends teased her to try. *A year ago I worried about bad hair days*, she thought. *Now it's no hair days.*

The mirror refogged. Angela wiped it again, this time to stare at her eyes. *I wonder if I'll be alive in a year.*

☑ Read Romans 8:18–27. Why don't problems go away?

Life isn't a sitcom where every difficulty ends in hugs and smiles and apologies within a half hour. And the future is like a fogged-up mirror. It's hard to see anything clearly. But you have to try.

God promises an eternity in heaven with no danger, death, disease, discomfort, or displeasure. And no dorks (Revelation 21:1–8).

Life here, however, can be a disaster. The world is decaying, falling apart, filled with moaning. Believers groan because we wait for a perfect world. Creation itself—everything God made—groans like a woman in labor, screaming with frustration to give birth to a renewed, perfected planet. And God's Holy Spirit groans as He prays ("intercedes") through us for God's perfect will for us.

That's foggy stuff. What we see, though, is that the world is out of whack. Life at its best is less than perfect. People sin, and creation produces things like mosquitoes, hurricanes, and cancer. Life at its worst is ghastly. And our best efforts to fix things are like wigs. They cover up the problem, but they don't grow new hair.

Our problems won't be solved completely until our "adoption as sons" (and daughters) at the end of time when God shakes the world, when He eliminates what is evil and perfects what belongs to Him. That's what we hope for. That's what God promised us when we became believers.

And so we wait.

I consider that our present sufferings are not worth comparing with the glory that will be revealed in us.

ROMANS 8:18

PART 4

Braving the HEAT

36

Du U Want 2 B ResQ'd r BarBQ'd?

Knock, knock. Bamm. BAMM. You open the door to your bullet-riddled apartment in a high-rise housing project. A fireman stands at your door.

"Excuse me," he says with polite urgency. "This building is on fire. You must have noticed the flames and heat and smoke from below. I'm here to rescue you."

"Actually, I hadn't noticed," you reply. "We're having a party."

"In there? In that smoke?" Your living room is a cloud from the waist up.

"Smoke? What smoke?" You cough as you finish pouring yourself a soda.

"I can hardly see your guests. And look—the heat's melted your ice."

"Well, you're bothering me and I don't want to leave. Everything I need is here."

"You don't understand. This building is burning down. I can show you the only way out. Just follow . . ." *Slam.*

▶ **Read Exodus 6:6–12. What did the Israelites think of the message Moses brought about God's plan to rescue them?**

For years Israel had rotted in slavery, a life "bitter with hard labor" (Exodus 1:14). Egyptian masters beat them to make bricks for the Pharoahs' building projects, and even tried to kill the Israelites' baby boys to prevent them from revolting as grown men.

Along came Moses, God's appointed leader. He brought a promise from God to save the Israelites from slavery, judge their masters, and guide them into a prosperous new land where they could live in peace as His people.

Here's the surprise: They didn't jump up and down with delight.

You might have the same reaction when God promises to bring you into a deep relationship with himself: *God, you couldn't possibly love me.* You're convinced you're too awful for God to love. *My life is too big of a mess.* You think your situation is too tough. *You don't care.* You suppose God doesn't understand the pressures you face. Or you may think, *Things are just great right here. My friends don't want to come with. It's bad, but it's home. I don't want to follow anyone. I don't know where God will take me.*

Here's another surprise: None of those feelings change the fact that God wants to help.

Moses reported this to the Israelites, but they did not listen to him because of their discouragement and cruel bondage.

EXODUS 6:9

37

Move It or Lose It

A message that passed secretly through camp told the prisoners to prepare to flee camp soon. And one night the POWs jolted awake as jets streaked over the camp an hour before dawn, destroying guard towers and the camp command. Half an hour later paratroopers stormed the prison itself. Cell doors swung open. The POWs were free. But they needed to walk out.

Crazed with fear, some prisoners wouldn't leave their cells. "We can't go out with no weapons! We're going to die!"

"Get out!" yelled the paratroopers, who knew they controlled the camp and a corridor to safety. "Trust us. Shut up and move!"

📝 **Read Exodus 14:10–18. What did God say to the Israelites when they thought they would die trying to escape slavery?**

God sent horrible plagues—frogs, gnats, hail, and death—to force the Egyptians to free their Israelite slaves. And He had more miracles in store—like parting the Red Sea and drowning the Egyptian army. When Israel still doubted God knew what He was doing, He told them, "I mean it. I'll save you. Quit moaning and start walking."

To escape, they had to believe God. And they had to act on what they believed.

In Christ, God acted to rescue you. Christ died to bring forgiveness and a life close to God. But you won't ever feel freedom if you don't believe Him and act on what you believe. You've got to get out of your cell.

First you watch. You see His power. You put your trust in Him.

Then you walk. You grab hold of what He's done for you. If you believe that God has forgiven and accepted you, then you talk to Him confidently (Hebrews 10:19–22). If you're sure God protects you, then you fear nothing (Psalm 118:6). If you know that hardship is God's discipline, then you resolve to learn from what you can't change (Hebrews 12:11). If you accept God's love for you, then you love others (1 John 4:19). If you trust that God wants what's best for you, then you obey (Psalm 19:7–11).

If you don't act on good news it can't change your life.

———————

Then the LORD said to Moses, "Why are you crying out to me? Tell the Israelites to move on."

EXODUS 14:15

38

Show Me the Way

David's parents wondered why he had helped himself to a clutch full of cash from a teacher's purse. "She's really stupid," he told them. "She always leaves her purse out."

"It sounds like you're trying to blame *her*," his dad replied. "David, the main thing we want to know is why you took the money."

"I didn't do it for myself. There's this girl I know whose coat was swiped. It wasn't fair. Our teacher knew it and didn't figure out who took it. I was sort of getting her back. I gave most of the money to this girl so she could get a new coat."

"David, don't you realize that was wrong?"

"But I only kept five bucks. That makes it not so bad, doesn't it?"

📭 **Read Exodus 13:21–22: Why did God show up in a pillar of cloud and of fire for Israel?**

God didn't abandon the Israelites to wander alone through the desert in search of the land He had promised them. He appeared by day in a pillar of cloud and by night in a pillar of fire, a visible sign of His presence and protection. The people followed the pillar as it moved. It cleared their confusion and built their confidence.

God didn't stop at pointing out a route and rest stops. On a mountaintop He spoke to Moses and revealed ten commands and other rules that told Israel how to act toward Him and toward people (Exodus 20:1–17). After Israel entered the land, God continued to speak through His spokespersons, the prophets.

We need the same assurance about where to go—how to live, what to do, and what not to do. It's not that we're dumb. But we need help to think right about wrong. Lying is bad, but we still find reasons to fib, exaggerate, jumble, and distort. Stealing is crooked, but we excuse ourselves when we shoplift, copy homework, or pirate software and tapes. Spin us around once and we're lost.

God doesn't dress in a cloud anymore, but He still guides us. He's given us the Bible to lead us where He wants to take us, to give us sure direction (2 Timothy 3:16). It's our map. Don't leave home without it.

By day the LORD went ahead of them in a pillar of cloud to guide them on their way and by night in a pillar of fire to give them light, so that they could travel by day or night.

EXODUS 13:21

39

Just What You Need

Maurita screamed as Val walked away, "I don't know why I tell you anything. You always talk behind my back."

Val had been Maurita's best friend since kindergarten. At their small school where everybody knew everybody—and everybody more or less hated everybody—they didn't have many other friends. When Val walked off, Maurita felt abandoned. Val was all she had. Where would she find a friend like her?

When a girl moved in next door, Maurita's hopes rose. But that went nowhere.

Then Maurita's math teacher paired her as a study partner with the girl who sat behind her. Jen was quiet, so Maurita didn't know her well. She was nice.

After a few months Jen became a better friend for Maurita than Val ever was.

📝 **Read Exodus 16:9–20. How did God provide for the Israelites when they thought they would starve in the desert?**

Not long after the Israelites fled slavery they faced certain starvation in the desert. Where could they find food for two million people? They didn't expect it to fall from the sky.

It did. God sent "manna" (which means "What is it?"). It was God's unexpected solution to an impossible problem, a sign that God was looking out for them. If they didn't trust that God would provide again the next day, what they hoarded overnight stunk and crawled with maggots. God made them gather manna repeatedly to remind them that they needed Him every day.

You face times when you think you're going to die—that you're going to wither with loneliness, shatter from stress, melt with nervousness. One more ounce of pressure and you'll crumple. You know you need God. Yet you can't see a solution coming.

God will take care of you. Among other things, God promises to provide godly friends (1 Kings 19:14–21), encouragement (2 Thessalonians 2:16–17), and peace (Philippians 4:6–7), and to meet your physical needs (Philippians 4:19).

Where will help come from? God. What will it be? You never know. When will it come? On time.

Expect it.

When the dew was gone, thin flakes like frost on the ground appeared on the desert floor. When the Israelites saw it, they said to each other, "What is it?" For they did not know what it was. Moses said to them, "It is the bread the LORD has given you to eat."

EXODUS 16:14–15

40
Out Your Nose

Neil sat in the hall after Mr. Holtz booted him from Sunday school class. After a while Mr. Holtz came out and asked Neil what was going on with him in class.

"I'm bored," Neil answered. "I've been coming to this church for seven years, and I can't make friends here."

"Do you have friends at school?"

"Lots."

"What are your friends like at school?"

"They're fun. I suppose we get in trouble sometimes. But they aren't boring like kids here. My friends there are cool."

📰 **Read Numbers 11:4–6, 18–20, and 31–34. What did the Israelites think of the food God miraculously provided for them in the desert?**

Sure, God gave manna, the Israelites thought. *"It's good fur yah,"* He says. *But the same stuff day after day? Bet God doesn't eat banana muffins three times a day.* The Israelites' minds cooked up pots of fish, and their memories picked fresh fruits and veggies. They wanted Egypt.

What they remembered, though, was unbelievably better than what they ever actually had. And heading back to slavery in order to enjoy a bag of onions was like wishing to be a dog locked in the pound because the biscuits taste good.

For a month God granted their request—meat—enough meat so that it came "out of their nostrils." God wasn't upset that His people were tired of the same food. He was angry because they would rather be bound as slaves than walk with Him. Their complaints rejected not only God's gift of food but God himself.

God gives gifts—family, church, work, school—meant only for your best (James 1:17). Your attitude toward what God gives—however plain, simple, or even boring God's gifts seem—reveals your attitude toward God himself (Exodus 16:4).

Don't whine for things your imagination claims are better than God's gifts. God may give you what you want. You know how pleasant it feels when you spit milk through your nose. Imagine hunks of bird meat touring your nasal cavity.

———

"But now we have lost our appetite; we never see anything but this manna!"

Numbers 11:6

41
Scared Off

During the trip with the kids from church, God seemed so real. So close. Everything made sense. Nothing, you decided, would come between you and God again. You wanted to trust and obey Him the best you knew how. You were so sure.

But the last night of the trip you dreamed about your friends back home. The dream was like a normal day at school, except that every few minutes a friend told you what they thought about your faith in God— *You think you're better than us. That stuff isn't real. You were just hyper—you would have signed up for the circus. Those people brainwashed you. Christians are geeks. Don't you know that being different is the kiss of death? I wouldn't say this if I didn't care about you, but . . .*

By the time you woke up you weren't so sure anymore. That day your own brain chimed in: *My friends are going to stop calling me. How will I survive at school? Everyone will make fun of me. Or ignore me.*

☛ **Read Numbers 13:26–33. What did the Israelite spies tell people about the land they saw?**

When God brought the Israelites to the border of the land He wanted to give them, twelve men went

97

ahead to spy out the land. It was as good as God said, spilling milk and honey, bursting with globs of grapes so huge they took two men to carry. The spies saw definite possibilities.

Even so, ten of the spies focused on the problem: The thugs who ran the land. They forgot God's promise: The land was theirs for the taking. True, there were giants. But God said the Israelites could whip them, not with their own skill but with His strength.

There's no doubt that what God promises us is good. We look at it, we want it: Friendship with the living God. Membership in His kingdom. Guidance and peace even in the middle of chaos. God's security, satisfaction, and splendor look mighty fine.

It's the giants that are scary—our friends' reactions, what we know God tells us to give up, our fears and weaknesses.

Our eyes are fine. It's our hearts that fail.

Yes, there are giants in the land. But God is bigger.

And they spread among the Israelites a bad report about the land they had explored. They said, "The land we explored devours those living in it. All the people we saw there are of great size."

NUMBERS 13:32

42

Stick Together or Get Stuck

The football team lined the wall of the middle school's main hall, looking cool on the first day of school. As Scott limped past, the team captain crooked his arm, cocked his head, opened his mouth, and lopped out his tongue. "Look, guys," Rick said as he drooled. "The retard is back! Everybody wave to the retard." The whole team copied Rick's cruel imitation.

Scott wasn't mentally retarded. Cerebral palsy slurred his speech and gave him little control over his muscles.

Not everyone thought Rick was funny. When he chased Scott down the hall, Rick's girl friend stuck out her foot and Rick sprawled. "I'm sick of you making fun of Scott," she yelled at him as he lay on the ground. "You're so mean!"

Question: You're one of the guys on the football team. Do you applaud as Rick's girl friend stomps on his chest?

▶ **Read Numbers 14:1–9. How did Caleb and Joshua and Aaron and Moses manage to stick up for what was right?**

It's great to decide to stand apart from the crowd.

But it's a lot more realistic to decide which crowd you want to stand with.

Everywhere you go you see two types of people. The first kind tries to do right. At school they want to learn, listen, do well. They treat others the way they want to be treated. At home they respect their families. At church they study to know God better and live what they know.

The other kind tests the limits. They do as much as they can get away with without getting busted.

It's true that the second group is often bigger. And that they carry rocks.

That doesn't mean they're right, or that they'll win. Joshua and Caleb stood up against popular opinion. They ripped their clothing to mourn the sinfulness of the others. They stood for God. They stood *together*. And because they did what God wanted, He made them leaders of a new, younger generation that stormed the Promised Land.

You may not have the guts to start the right crowd. But find a way to join them.

Joshua son of Nun and Caleb son of Jephunneh, who were among those who had explored the land, tore their clothes and said to the entire Israelite assembly, "The land we passed through and explored is exceedingly good."

NUMBERS 14:6–7

43

What You Want Is What You Get

At her clinic appointment she screamed and cried. "NO! The test must be wrong!" In the next months as her stomach grew she couldn't deny what she had done. On due day, when her abdomen wrenched with labor pains she knew there was no easy escape.

That pain was nothing compared to having her baby whisked away to its adoptive parents. It was a perfect baby boy, the doctor said, but she didn't get to see him. Putting her baby up for adoption meant she could finish school and get on with life. But she wondered a hundred times a day what he was doing and how he was.

Even years later when she had a husband and family she still imagined what the boy looked like, and pretended he was taking his spot at the table when she called for dinner.

▶ **Read Numbers 14:26–35. What happened to the Israelites when they decided to disobey God over and over?**

When you rough up your little brother in the living room and knock a knickknack off a shelf, sometimes you can glue the pieces together. But the knickknack you whacked won't ever be what it used to be. At best, it's cracked.

God does better than we can. When we sin and whack our relationship with God off the shelf, accepting God's offer of forgiveness mends the cracks. God fixes our relationship. The cracks vanish.

The Israelites, God said, sinned against Him over and over (Numbers 14:22). When they refused to storm the land and accused God of plotting to murder them and their children in the wilderness—they even vowed to choose a new leader and return to bondage in Egypt—God was beyond furious. "How long will these people treat me with contempt?" He asked. "How long will they refuse to believe in me, in spite of all the miraculous signs I have performed among them?" (Numbers 14:11).

Moses pleaded with God, and God forgave the Israelites (Numbers 14:20).

So they lived happily ever after, right?

Not quite. Forgiveness doesn't eliminate the results of sinful actions. Their guilt was gone. The consequences weren't. God gave the people what they asked for.

He locked them out of the land. They missed the best of what He planned.

———————

So tell them, "As surely as I live, declares the LORD, I will do to you the very things I heard you say: In this desert your bodies will fall—every one of you twenty years old or more . . . who has grumbled against me."

NUMBERS 14:28–29

44

Comfy Cozy

Legs and arms flow in perfect harmony, a symphony of coordination and grace. As you admire your powerful stride you hum the tune "O Lord, it's hard to be humble, when you're perfect in every way."

Glancing over your shoulder you discover you're so far ahead of the pack that you decide to stop running. You congratulate yourself. *I deserve a break. Been training hard, looking fine. Yep, I'm good. So good.* You plop on the track and spread out your picnic. You bite into your hero sandwich. *Hero*—how appropriate, you think.

You lie back and fall into a deep slumber, dreaming of the gold medals and world records you're sure you'll win.

Sleeping contentedly, you rouse only when a truck driver rolls down his window and yells, "Hey, moron! Get outta the road!"

▶ **Read Deuteronomy 8:6–20. Why did God warn Israel against getting comfortable when things went well?**

God saved Israel from some tough stuff—slavery, snakes, scorpions, and starvation, for starters. And the homeland He planned for them was sweet—filled with streams and springs, wheat and barley, grapes, figs, honey, sheep, silver, and gold.

God worried that His people would forget all about Him when they settled in such a nice place.

It's no problem remembering God when life goes bad. You pray, you complain, you cry for comfort. But when you feel safe and satisfied, you're easily distracted, wrapped up in what He gives you, caught comparing yourself to others. You're not alert and on-track. You forget that everything you have and are comes from God (James 1:17, 1 Corinthians 4:7). You dream that you've arrived at the finish line.

But your pace will speed up when you rouse yourself with the fact that God is still God, worth thanking and chasing even when life goes great.

The risk in slowing your pace in the race isn't that other runners—other believers—will pass you by. The real danger is that your pride will run you over.

When you have eaten and are satisfied, praise the LORD your God for the good land he has given you. Be careful that you do not forget the LORD your God, failing to observe his commands. . . .

DEUTERONOMY 8:10–11

45
I Smell a Skunk

"Thawr's skuhnk in thuh pawrk, yuh know."

Skunks? *Yeah, right*, you laugh as you walk away. You aren't about to let a stupid park ranger ruin your fun. Anyone who talks that dumb *is* that dumb, you figure. So you ignore his advice to keep food in sealed containers inside a car so raccoons or skunks—or bear—don't ravage your camp.

You were a long way from believing the ranger. Before bed you spilled chips and splashed soda inside and out of your tent, and tucked yourself in with a stash of candy under your pillow.

As soon as you lay quiet you noticed animal noises in the woods. *Maybe that dumb ranger knew what he was talking about. Nah.* But you hid in your sleeping bag when the scratching started on the side of your tent, and you ran for your car when you heard claws ripping nylon.

Read Judges 2:6–15. Why didn't Israel rest easy in the land God had promised them?

As God had said, the Israelites who refused to enter the land died in the desert. Their children became the heroes—conquering most of the peoples in the land. In time, though, a generation grew up that hadn't seen

God's miracles firsthand. That's when the trouble began.

Instead of serving God, this new generation of Israelites followed the gods of their neighbors, *baals*, who were worshiped through prostitution and child sacrifice. When God saw Israel's disobedience, He allowed their sinful neighbors to survive. He let their presence test Israel, to see if they would follow God or turn away.

Because Israel let sin stick around, sin became a sticky mess for them.

Doing wrong hurts you now. It's like choosing to get beat up. But it also hurts you later. God wants to chase sin from your life by changing how you think and act. When you don't let Him, you let your enemy live. It threatens you. It teases you. And sometimes it wallops you all over again. God doesn't warn you for nothing.

Don't be surprised if you don't get the sugar out of your tent and you wake up with a skunk on your head.

After that whole generation had been gathered to their fathers, another generation grew up, who knew neither the LORD nor what he had done for Israel. Then the Israelites did evil in the eyes of the LORD and served the Baals.

JUDGES 2:10–11

46
Onward

You spent the past week scribbling in yearbooks—things like *"You're a great person. Don't ever change."* Or *"Remember to call."* Sometimes you signed your name with *"F/F"* ("Friends Forever").

Gag. You didn't mean nine-tenths of that stuff. You wanted gobs of signatures in your yearbook, so you had to write something in other people's books.

Then eighth grade graduation shook your brain awake. Middle school meant more than what you were scrawling in yearbooks. Because of middle school, life would never be the same. You started as goofy post-elementary kids, but you weren't kids anymore. You had made the grade and were moving up. You had a future to build.

Suddenly you started to miss the place. It actually seemed pretty good.

But you also looked forward to something more.

▶ **Read Deuteronomy 4:32–40.**

The Israelites were camped at the edge of the land God had promised, ready to enter. What did Moses want them to remember?

When Israel looked back at forty years of wandering in the wilderness, they had no problem recalling the difficulties they faced in the desert.

Moses feared they might forget how good God had been—and that God's goodness should make a difference in their lives.

The world had never seen anything like God's friendship with Israel. God conversed with them, and through pests and floods and fire and miracles, He rescued them from slavery to make them His people.

They had only begun to see what God would do. And what God had done for them, Moses said, should change their lives. They had seen that God was God. Now they should follow Him.

God's acts were real, not mush made up to write in someone's yearbook. God's love for you is just as real. Through Christ He acted to rescue you. He's promised to never leave you.

What you've learned about God so far is just the beginning. And it should change you. God is God. Follow Him.

———————

You were shown these things so that you might know that the LORD is God; besides him there is no other.

DEUTERONOMY 4:35

Acknowledgments

Thank you first of all to Lyn, Nate, and Karin for running God's race with me. Thank you to Dad and Mom and Tom and Pat and our families for sanity visits and phone calls.

Thanks to old friends for staying close and kind: Randy and Mary Horn, Dick and Carolyn Lee, Maurice and Beth Lee, Jim and Joanie Maines, Jim and Anne Papandrea, and Todd and Sally Wessman.

Thanks to the Monday morning biscuit and Bible bunch—Paul Hypki, John Mackett, Fred Snyder, and Dick Wittow. May we discover both God and a restaurant free of elevator music.

Thanks to Wendy Davis, Justin Beckman, and Mark Seversen for help with writing, and to Barb Lilland and Bethany House Publishers for encouragement and sharp editing and production.

We're strangers (Hebrews 11:13–16). But we get to run together.

Kevin Walter Johnson